Stock Investors
Technology Manual

Stock Investors Technology Manual

Robert Fox

Writers Club Press
San Jose New York Lincoln Shanghai

Stock Investors
Technology Manual

Writers Club Press
an imprint of iUniverse.com, Inc.

For information address:
iUniverse.com, Inc.
5220 S 16th, Ste. 200
Lincoln, NE 68512
www.iuniverse.com

ISBN: 0-595-15366-6

Printed in the United States of America

The Cash Account

THE CASH ACCOUNT

First, decide which company's stock you would like to invest in and contact your broker or place your on line order. The day you place your BUY ORDER is known as the TRADE DATE. Three business days after you place your BUY ORDER is known as the SETTL-MENT DATE. You should receive a confirmation, confirming that your buy order has been finalized by the SETTLEMENT DATE.

After you check your confirmation for accuracy, you must pay for your trade in full. This means paying one hundred percent of the purchase price plus any commissions due. If you do not require having funds on deposit in your account and failing to meet the payment after settlement date, you may be entitled to an extension of time. Extensions are granted for reasons such as check in the mail and a variety of other good excuses. But if you still do not have your payment available for your purchase when your extension expires, your purchase will be sold at the market, meaning at the current market price at the time of the sell out not the purchase price you bought the stock for, and you will be responsible for any losses sustained due to such a transaction.

The cash account is so easy to understand that we could sum it up as easy as this:

TRADE DATE: The date that you place an order to buy stock

3

SETTLEMENT DATE: The date that your buy trade is finalized.

CONFIRMATION: This confirms that your purchase (number of shares purchased, at what dollar amount per share plus commissions due).

EXTENSION: Extension of time permitted for late payment if necessary.

The rules and regulations are quite similar when it comes to selling stock in a cash account. There's a TRADE DATE, the date you place your order to sell your stock at the market and there's a settlement date, the day your sale is finalized. You will also receive a CONFIRMATION confirming your sell order.

As you can determine, the rules and regulations for trading on a CASH ACCOUNT are simple to say the least. So let's move on and see how a stock investor uses the CASH ACCOUNT as a tool to purchase and sell stock, build a stock portfolio and measure gains and losses.

Just a note, although your purchase of stock settles three days after the trade date, your payment isn't due until the fifth business day after trade date or two days after settlement date which is the same thing. If your payment is not received by this target date, then you could be eligible for an extension of time. As mentioned, extensions are granted according to the reason payment is late such as check in the mail.

Next, let's get familiar with the terminology used when discussing your porfolio. This will make reading this book as well as discussing your portfolio with your stockbroker a lot easier.

TERMINOLOGY

CREDIT BALANCE: The sum of cash held in your cash account that is owed to you.

DEBIT BALANCE: The sum of money owed to your cash account.

MARKET VALUE: The total net worth of stock held in your cash account regardless of whether you have paid for it or not at the present time.

LONG POSITION: Denomination of shares of a certain stock held in your cash account.
For example: 100 shares of XYZ corp.

SHORT POSITION: Denomination of shares of a certain stock owed to your account.

EQUITY: The intrinsic value or overall value of the cash account owned by you minus any debits and short positions (as defined above) and excluding any stock that has not been paid for as yet.

The terminology used to discuss a portfolio that trades on margin is available in the chapter devoted to the margin account.

READING A CASH ACCOUNT

Obvious as it is, the way to profit from trading on a cash account is to buy low and sell high. The following examples show how a cash account may read using the buy low and sell high method utilizing the terminology listed above.

Let's assume for example that you decide to invest in XYZ Corp. stock selling at the current market price of $25 pre share. Your cash account will read as follows:

LONG: 100 (shares) XYZ Corp. (name of stock) @25(price per share)

MARKET VALUE: $2,500(100 shares times price per share $25)

DEBIT BALANCE: $2,500(Dollar amount owed on purchase)

EQUITY: -0- (Value of stock owned)

Now let's further assume that time has passed since you've placed your order to purchase stock in your cash account. Naturally you paid for your purchase on a timely basis and hopefully the price per share of your purchase has increased.

For the sake of our example, let's assume that the price per share of your investment has increased from $25 per share to $30 per share. Your cash account would now read as follows:

LONG: 100 XYZ Corp. @$30

MARKET VALUE: $3,000

EQUITY: $3,000

Notice how the market value has increased from $2,500 to $3,000 due to the increase in price per share from $25 to $30. Also, you now have equity ($3,000) instead of a debit balance ($2500) because you paid for your purchase and now own the stock one hundred per cent.

This theory can also have a reverse affect meaning, even though your intensions are to buy low and sell high, the stock you purchase may actually start to drop in price per share. Continuing with our example, let's assume that the price per share of your purchase has decreased from $25 per share (the original purchase price) to $20 per share. Your cash account would read as follows:

LONG: 100 XYZ Corp. @20

MARKET VALUE: $2000

EQUITY: $2,000

This can happen to anyone, any investment and, at any time. If you were to sell your investment at this time, you would avoid any further loss if the price per share of this stock were to continue to decrease. But the original loss incurred ($500) would still in fact apply.

WHEN CAN I TAKE MY PROFIT?

If you are fortunate enough to invest in a stock that increases in price per share instead of the other way around and decide that you would like to sell your investment in order to reap the profits from it, then you simply have to place an order to sell.

Going back to our original example (the price per share increasing from $25 to $30) and assuming that you have placed an order to sell your stock, your cash account would now read as follows:

CREDIT BALANCE: $3,000

EQUITY: $3,000

Since your equity has increased from $2,500 to $3,000, you have just profited from your investment by $500. Note: this example does not reflect any commissions due on the sale of this stock. Oh yes, by the way you will be charged commissions on the sale of the stock that you paid commissions on when you originally purchased it. It may not seem fair to the stock investor but it's a win win situation for the broker on hand as you pay these commissions whether or not you profit or incur a loss on each sale.

PROFITTING FROM
LONG TERM INVESTMENTS

The previous example showed how you could make a profit investing in stock using the buy low sell high theory. But, the example was timeless, there was no specific time table involved showing a specific trade date of the purchase verses any specific trade date of the sale.

This example could have taken place over a one-week period or many months later. Although any stock investor would wish for every trade made to be a profitable one in the least amount of time possible, the reality of investing in stock is that time and good solid investments are what it takes to benefit most by investing in stock.

Buying low and selling high is not the only way to benefit from investing in stock.

When choosing your investments it is wise to consider annual dividends that the stock you are investing in may pay.

Utility stocks such as Electric companies or Natural Gas companies usually pay dividends on an annual basis. These are known as *INCOME STOCKS* and may pay for themselves in the long run. This is not a plug for utility stocks, please consult a competent professional before investing in types of securities mentioned hereafter.

Here's an example of how income stocks pay for themselves when considering long-term investments. Let's assume that you purchase two hundred shares of ABC stock at fifteen dollars per share. Your total cost for that purchase would be three thousand dollars.

Let's assume further that ABC stock was paying an annual dividend of two dollars and fifty cents per share. Since you own two hundred shares of ABC stock, that would entitle you to a cash dividend of five hundred dollars annually (200 shares times $2.50 dividend per share).

If you were to hold on to your two hundred shares of ABC stock for ten years and receiving annual cash dividends over this ten-year period, you would have accumulated a dividend income of five thousand dollars. Do the math:

200 shares ABC Corp times $2.50 annual dividend per year = $500

$500 collected annually for ten years = $5000

The original purchase price for two hundred shares of ABC Corp. was three thousand dollars; your accumulated annual cash dividend income was five thousand dollars. This investment paid for itself and netted you another two thousand dollars profit not to mention that the price per share may have also increased since your original investment.

But, cash dividends and price per share increases are not all you should consider when it comes to long term investing. You should also consider the possibility of stock splits.

STOCK SPLITS

Another advantage to long-term investing is stock splits. Commonly a stock split will take place when a company wants to attract more investors by issuing more shares of the company's stock to the public at a lower price per share than the current market price.

Naturally a company cannot call a share holders meeting and declare that their shares of that company's stock will now be worth half of what the current market price per share is in order to attract new investors. But by splitting the stock, this can be achieved without any of the current shareholders losing any of their investments.

EXAMPLE: ABC Company has announced a TWO for ONE stock split which means that for every one share of stock you own at fifty dollars per share, for example, they will take away one share of stock and replace it with two shares of the same stock valued at half the price per share than the original stock.

Before the split your cash account reads:

LONG: 100 ABC @50

MARKET VALUE: $5000

EQUTY: $5000

After the split your cash account will read:

LONG: 200 ABC @25

MARKET VALUE: $5000

EQUTY: $5000

Although the original shareholder now has twice as much stock long on his or her account, the market value remains the same because the price per share of the stock has been adjusted from fifty dollars per share to twenty-five dollars per share.

The new lower price per share will attract new investors or even encourage current shareholders to invest more in this stock thus increasing the price per share. And, with the new price increases and you as the investor now owning twice as many share as originally purchased, can in fact now double your potential profits.

BUILDING A DIVERSE STOCK PORTFOLIO

It is wise to build a diverse stock portfolio consisting of numerous companies stocks. Investing in one company's stock alone is known as concentrated investing. Concentrated investing is risky due to the unpredictable fluctuation in the stock market as well as the unpredictability of any one company's stability.

If an investor had five hundred dollars to invest in the stock market and decided to invest the whole five hundred thousand dollars into one stock, his or her cash account, after paying for the initial trade, may look something like this:

LONG: 10,000 XYZ Corp. @5

MARKET VALUE: $500,000

EQUITY: $500,000

This may look like an easy and sensible way to make a quick fortune because, if the underlying stock were to increase by just one dollar, than the investor would make a cool one hundred dollar profit.

The cash account would now read as follows:

LONG: 10,000 XYZ Corp. @6

MARKET VALUE: $600,000

EQUITY: $600,000

This looks like a great way to make a quick fortune if the stock market works in your favor and drives the price per share up and not the other way around. Let's take a look at how the same cash account would look if the stock market were to swing the other way, DOWN.

The cash account would read as follows:

LONG: 10,000 XYZ Corp, @4

MARKET VALUE: $400,000

Equity: $400,000

The initial investment of five hundred thousand dollars has just taken a hit by one dollar per share reducing the market value of the initial investment by one hundred thousand dollars. Still further, what if the same investment took a two-dollar per share hit.
Your loss would be a substantial two hundred thousand dollars.

The cash account would read as follows:

LONG: 10,000Corp. @3

MARKET VALUE: $300,000

EQUTY: $300,000

This is why concentrated investing is an extremely risky type of investing. Although using five hundred thousand dollar investment may seem a bit extreme, it is wise to consider that a stock investor who has a considerably less money to invest can feel the same sting if his or her concentrated investments price per share dropped by a measly one dollar.

THE DIVERSE CASH ACCOUNT

Building a diverse cash account portfolio reduces the risk of losing a fortune overnight as seen in the preceding examples, but it can't eliminate this risk. Anyone at anytime can suffer the ill effects of a down market regardless of how you invest (concentrated or diverse).

Diversifying your cash account portfolio is a way of hedging against an overall loss to your investments. The previous examples showed how a concentrated portfolio could make or break a stock investor. So, now let's see how a diversified cash account portfolio can hedge against a major loss with the following examples:

CASH ACCOUNT:

JAN. 1st:

LONG: 100 ABC @10
             100 EFG @ 5 ½
             200 XYZ @ 7

M.V. $2,950

Now let's assume that one months time has passed and the price per share of the securities held in your portfolio has fluctuated

FEB. 1ˢᵗ:

LONG: 100 ABC @7
        100 EFG @ 7 ½
        200 XYZ @ 8

M.V. $3,050

As you can see that after one month's time of fluctuating stock prices, one of the securities price per share has dropped by two points ($2) but, this will not have an adverse effect on the overall value of the portfolio because the other two securities have increased in price per share hedging against such a loss.

This is the safeguard that you should look for when building a stock portfolio in a cash account.

TAKING DELIVERY OF YOUR STOCK

After you have paid for the purchase of your stock it will be held long in your cash account. The terminology for this is called *STREET NAME STOCK* or stock held in *SEGRAGATION* or *SEG*.

These terminologies simple mean that the stock you purchased is not held in your name although you are the true owner. There is no physical certificate with your name on it attesting to the number of share you purchased. Instead, your purchase, long in the cash account, reads as a book entry backed up by shares of a particular security held by the brokerage company that you do business with.

This is a secure way to build a stock portfolio because there is no certificate to lose or be eaten by the family dog. It also simplifies sale transactions when it comes time to sell your stock especially for short-term investments.

Although holding stock in *STREET NAME* is common practice and highly recommended, you may have reason to take delivery of your stock. You may want to present it to somebody as a present or use it as collateral to secure a loan at a bank or another brokerage company or maybe you just prefer to hold the certificate(s) in your possession.

If you prefer to take delivery of your stock, your broker or broker-age company that you do business with will submit your request to a transfer agent who will in tern register the stock in your name and issue you a stock certificate.

After the certificate has been issued, you can have it mailed directly to your home, business or to where ever except a post office box because the certificate will be insured and must be signed for or you can elect to have it mailed back to your brokerage company and have them hold it in *SAFEKEEPING*.

Holding your certificate in safekeeping means that the brokerage company that you do business with will hold the certificate in their vault. This will reduce the risk of loss due to misplacement, carelessness' or even hungry dogs.

SELLING STOCK IN YOUR NAME

If you are planning to sell stock held in your name then you should pay your stock broker a visit so that he or she can deposit the stock into a cash account and place the order to sell it. But if this situation presents a problem such as your stock broker is in another city or state or you need to place a sell order right away to prevent opportunity lost, you can simple phone in your sell order to your stock broker and follow up your transaction with a visit on a future date or mail the certificate in to your stock broker.

Do not mail stock certificates directly to the company that you have invested in or to the transfer agent. The certificate must be mailed or brought in to the stockbroker in order to satisfy a short position now created in your ash account.

Example: (The Cash Account will read)

May 1st:

SOLD: 100 XYZ Co. @10

SHORT: 100 XYZ Co.

M.V.   −$1,000

EQUITY: *0*

CREDIT BALACE: $1,000

Notice how the market value reflects a minus sign (-) and your equity is zero even though you sold stock that you own and the cash account reflects a credit balance of one thousand dollars. This is due to the fact that your stockbroker has not taken delivery of your stock certificate.

Once your stockbroker takes delivery of your stock, your cash account will read as follows:

May 3rd:

EQUITY: $1,000

CREDIT: $1,000

Now the credit balance created by the sale of your stock is available to you as long as you have signed the certificate before you mailed it to your stockbroker. If you neglected to sign your stock certificate before you mailed out and you cannot get to your stock brokers office to sign it, he or she can simply mail you a *STOCK POWER* which you can simple sign on the dotted line and return to your stock broker.

Your stock broker will then simple attach the Stock Power to the stock certificate now rendering it negotiable and freeing up the proceeds from the sale of your stock. You may want to consider asking your stockbroker to supply you with blank Stock Powers if you make a practice of selling stock in which you hold the certificate because like anything else the mail is not a secure and sure thing.

Mail can be misplaced or lost or even stolen and if that's the case you would not want the stock certificate to be in negotiable form with our signature on it. So you should send in the stock certificate unsigned followed by the Stock Power under separate cover.

WORKING WITH FRACTIONS

Some stock investors consider fractions an annoyance or to complicated to work with when figuring the value of a stock simple because they don't now how to reconfigure the fraction into decimals.

This can lead to inaccurate pricing because a lot of stock investors will round off the fraction to the whole. But, this problem can easily be resolved by making yourself a conversion chart that you can keep in your pocket, wallet, purse, desk or just about anywhere.

In order to make your conversion chart, all that you will require is a calculator and a little patience but not too much because this is going to be easier than you may thing.

In order to convert a fraction into a decimal you simply divide the first part of the fraction (the NUMERATOR) (A) which represents any number by the second part of the fraction (the DENOMINATOR) (B) which represents any number.

Example: A/B (fraction) A divided by B = the Decimal

1/8 (fraction) 1 divided 8 = .125 (decimal)

It's just a simple matter of division, which can be done in a split second using a calculator.

Let's try other examples:

¼   1 divided by 4 = .250

½   1 divided by 2 = .500

Using this simple mathematical equation will help you to create a Conversion Chart like the one on the following page.

CONVERSION CHART

FRACTIONS	DECIMALS
1/16	.0625
1/8	.125
3/16	.1875
¼	.250
5/16	.3125
3/8	.375
7/16	.4375
½	.500
9/16	.5625
5/8	.625
11/16	.5625
¾	.750

The Margin Account

THE MARGIN ACCOUNT

The margin account is very unique as it enables you to purchase twice as many shares of stock versus a dollar per dollar trade in the cash account. In other words, you can purchase two hundred shares of stock in the margin account and pay the equivalent of a purchase of one hundred shares of the same stock in the cash account.

Example:

Cash account: Purchase–200 ABC @10 = $2,000 : Equity $2,000

Margin account: Purchase–400 ABC @10 = $4,000 you pay $2,000 : Equity $2,000

When you purchase stock on MARGIN, you will be required to put up FIFTY PERCENT of the initial purchase price. This FIFTY PERCENT requirement is known as a FEDERAL CALL or terminologically know as a *FED CALL*.

A Fed Calls requirements are basically the same as the purchase of stock in the Cash account. There is a three day Settlement Date and payment is due by the fifth business day from Trade Date.

Another requirement is that you must pay fifty percent or two thousand dollars, which ever one is greater, for the initial (first time) purchase of stock on margin. This requirement satisfies yet another requirement which stipulates that an initial purchase on Margin must meet a Two Thousand Dollar *MINIMUM EQUITY REQUIREMENT*.

Example: Purchase–400 ABC @10 = $4,000 : FED CALL $2,000

After you deposit the two thousand dollars to your Margin account in order to meet the Fed Call, you will also have satisfied the two thousand dollar equity requirement.

But what if you purchase less shares of the same stock (as an initial purchase) at the same price. Your Margin requirements will read as follows:

Purchase–100 ABC @10 = $1,000 : FED CALL $500
Amount Required: $2,000 (to cover the minimum equity requirement).

Although the Fed Call will read $500 (fifty percent of the purchase price) you will still be required to deposit funds to your account totaling no less than two thousand dollars in order to meet the two thousand dollar minimum equity requirement.

If you were to make an initial purchase on Margin of the same stock but instead of four hundred shares or less (as used in the preceding examples), you decided to purchase eight hundred shares, your requirements will read as follows:

Purchase: 800 ABC @10 = $8,000 : FED CALL $4,000

The requirement on the initial purchase of eight hundred shares will be the dollar amount of the Fed Call "only", because payment of the Fed Call also satisfies the two thousand dollar Minimum Requirement.

At this point you may be wondering how you can get away with paying for just Fifty Percent of the purchase price of stock on margin as opposed to One Hundred Percent of the purchase of the same amount of shares in the cash account. The answer is simple, the margin account in it's own unique way, carries a debit balance as opposed to the cash account which requires One Hundred Percent payment on all purchases which in turn leaves the cash account to assume no debit balance after payment is received.

HOW DOES A MARGIN ACCOUNT CARRY A DEBIT BALANCE

Actually, what you are doing is borrowing fifty percent of the purchase price of the stock from the Brokerage Company that you do business with.

This is not like obtaining a Cash Loan from a bank, which would require you to pay off in monthly installments. A Debit Balance will remain on your Margin account for as long as you want to maintain a Debit Balance. Instead of paying it off like a loan from the bank, you will simple be charged monthly interest on the outstanding Debit Balance.

The amount of interest charged monthly to your Margin account will be determined by the amount of the Debit Balance that your Margin account carries. Margin Interest Rates are usually determined on a scale ranging from Two Thousand to Five Thousand dollars–Five Thousand to Ten Thousand dollars–Ten thousand to Twenty Thousand dollars and so on.

For example, if your margin debit was between the Five Thousand to Ten Thousand dollar scale, you may be charged One and a Half Percent interest on that debit according to the Interest Rate determined by the Brokerage Company that you do business with, and that rate is then times by the BROKER CALL RATE for that particular day.

This is how your Brokerage Company profits by lending you fifty percent of your investments value on Margin.

BENIFITING TWICE AS MUCH FROM A MARGIN ACCOUNT

Your account will be long twice as many shares for the same cash deposit as the cash account, which means your market value will be twice that of the cash account.

Your debit however, will not increase with the value of the stock long on margin excluding margin interest.

The following examples will demonstrate how you will profit twice as much by purchasing stock on margin.

CASH ACCOUNT:

Jan. 2

Purchase: 100 ABC @20

Debit: $2,000.00

Jan 9

Deposit: $2,000.00

Long: 100 ABC @20

Market Value: $2,000.00

Equity: $2,000.00

Jan. 23

Long: 100 ABC @23

Market Value: $ 2,300.00

Equity: $2,300.00

Notice that the price per share of the ABC stock has increased by three dollars per share. This increase in price per share has also increased the equity by three hundred dollars resulting in a profit to the investor.

If the investor purchased twice as many shares on margin and deposited the same two thousand dollars to cover the margin call, the profit to the investor would have been six hundred dollars, twice the profit generated by the cash account purchase.

MARGIN ACCOUNT:

Jan. 2

Purchase: 200 ABC @20

Debt: $4,000.00

Margin Call: $2,000.00

Jan 9

Deposit: $2,000.00

Long: 200 ABC @20

Market Value: $4,000.00

Debt: $2,000.00

Equity: $2,000.00

Jan. 23

Long: 200 ABC @23

Market Value: $4,600.00

Debit: $2,000.00

Equity: $2,600.00

Notice that the margin account now has equity of $2,600.00, which is an increase of six hundred dollars.

The profit on the margin account is double that of the profit on the cash account for obvious reasons, the margin account has twice as many shares long as opposed to the cash account.

Increasing market values are not the only ways to benefit from a margin account. Investing in stocks that pay annual dividends is another way to gain twice as much income as opposed to purchasing stock in a cash account.

Let's assume that ABC stock is paying a cash dividend of one dollar and twenty-five cents per share to its stockholders. If the investor purchased one hundred shares in the cash account, the stock brokerage company would credit the cash account, one hundred and twenty five dollars in dividends due the investor.

To arrive at the total dividend due the investor, just multiply the dividend of $1.25 times the amount of shares the investor is long, in this case one hundred shares, ($1.25 x 100 = $125.00).

On the other hand, if the investor had purchased two hundred shares on margin, the investor would have received a dividend credit to the margin account of two hundred and fifty dollars (1.25 x 200 = $250.00) twice the income received in the cash account.

Even though the investor borrowed half the value of the purchase price of the stock, the investor is entitled to tone hundred percent of all profits and dividends received to the margin account.

Let's build a margin portfolio from scratch to better understand the function of the margin account.

As discussed earlier, you will be required to deposit fifty percent of the purchase price of the stock you invest in, or two thousand dollars, which ever is greater.

After careful research with the guidance of your stockbroker, let's assume that you have decided to invest in two different companies. Your account will read as follows:

Jan. 2

Purchased: 200 ABC @20
           300 XYZ @5

Market Value: $5,500.00
Debit: $5,500.00
Margin Call: $2,750.00
Equity Call: -0-

After you have paid the margin call, your account will read as follows:

Long: 200 ABC @20
           300 XYZ @5

Market Value: $ 5,500.00

Debit: $2,750.00
Equity: $2,750.00
Equity %: 50 percent

To arrive at the Equity Percentage, use this simple formula. Divide your equity by your market value.

(Equity $2,750.00–M.V. $5,500.00 = .5 or 50%)

Let's assume that your investments have increased in price per share, your margin account will read as follows:

Jan. 15

Long: 200 ABC @22
          300 XYZ @7

Market Value: $6,500.00
Debit: $2,700.00
Equity: $3,800.00
Equity%:   58%
Margin Excess: $550.00
Buying Power: $1,100.00

Notice that your account equity percentage is at fifty eight percent and your margin account now reflects a margin excess and buying power figure.

To arrive at the margin excess figure, we use this simple formula:

EQUITY, MINUS 50% OF THE MARKET VALUE

(.5 X $6,500.00 = $3,250.00 or 50% of M.V.)
$3,800.00 (EQUITY)—$3,250.00 (50% of M.V. = $550.00 Excess).

To arrive at the figure for Buying Power, use this simple formula:

MARGIN ESCESS TIMES TWO = BUYING POWER

WHAT IS BUYING POWER?

As we discussed earlier, a margin account is designed to give you the opportunity to borrow against your stock investments.

When you established your margin account your margin account you were able to borrow fifty percent of your stocks market value. But now that your account has excess due to the increase in value of the price per share of your investment, you can borrow against the increased market value of your stocks.

This will give you're the opportunity to purchase more stock on your margin account without depositing any additional funds to your account.

In our example, with the margin excess figure of five hundred and fifty dollars, we now have a buying power of one thousand one hundred dollars, which is the total value of additional stock you can purchase on margin without depositing additional funds to your margin account.

USING YOUR BUYING POWER

Let's assume you decide to take advantage of your buying power and purchase an additional one hundred shares of XYZ stock at seven dollars per share.

Your margin account will read as follows:

Jan. 15

Purchase: 100 XYZ @7
Long: 200 ABC @22
             400 XYZ @7
Market Value: $7,200.00
Debit: $3,400.00
Equity: $3,800.00
Equity %: 52%
Margin Excess: $ 200.00
Buying Power: $ 400.00

You have just purchased additional stock to your margin account without depositing additional funds to your account to cover the purchase. You simply doubled your margin excess and exercised your right to use your buying power in order to purchase additional stock.

You may feel comfortable with your investments at this time and decide not to make any further investments until your buying power increases. But keep in mind that you can purchase as much stock as you wish on margin as long as you are willing to deposit funds to your account to cover any additional margin calls that may arise after you have exceeded your buying power.

The point is, you are not limited to the amount of stock you can purchase on margin by the buying power figure if you are willing to deposit additional funds to your account. Also, you are not limited to just purchasing stock by doubling the margin excess but you can borrow cash against one times the margin excess.

BORROWING CASH
AGAINST MARGIN

We have already established the fact that you can borrow up to fifty percent of the purchase price of the stock you wish to invest in but, if you are holding a stock certificate in your possession and deposit it to your margin account you can borrow up to fifty percent of its market value providing you do not exceed the two thousand dollar minimum equity requirement and providing the stock you are depositing is eligible for margin.

This means that if you deposit stock to your margin account worth four thousand dollars you will be able to borrow two thousand dollars against the stocks value.

If you were to deposit a stock certificate worth three thousand dollars, you would only be able to borrow up to one thousand dollars taking into consideration the two thousand dollar minimum equity requirement.

Keep in mind that if you decide to borrow cash against your stock, you will be charged margin interest once a month against the debit you create when the funds are paid out of your account the same as it is charged to your account when you create a debit by purchasing stock on margin.

WHAT HAPPENS
IN A DOWN MARKET?

During a down market, not all stocks decrease in value some stocks may actually increase in value. However, the majority of stocks do decrease in value and if you have a margin account with a portfolio made up of a variety of different stock positions (diversified account) then you can almost be certain that your margin account will be affected by a down market.

This is why understanding and knowing how to maintain your margin account is crucial knowledge that every investor should possess.

Unfortunately, a great number of stock investors do not possess this knowledge and find themselves in a frustrating situation when their stock broker calls and asks them to deposit additional funds to their margin account when the equity percentage of their margin account falls below the minimum equity percent allowed.

Do not confuse the minimum equity requirement with the minimum equity percentage. These are to entirely different requirements.

The minimum equity requirement reflects the minimum value of stock owned by the investor in terms of dollar amount. You must own a minimum total value of stock worth two thousand dollars or more.

To determine an equity percentage, we divide the equity by the market value and come up with a percentage figure and not a dollar amount.

After you have established a margin account, you will be required to maintain a minimum equity percentage.

The minimum equity percentage requirement is twenty five percent which most brokerage companies; if not all, will see the minimum equity requirement at thirty to thirty five percent and even forty percent for concentrated positions (one position long on a margin account). This is commonly known as house requirements or house calls the brokerage company you do business with being the house.

The reason for this is understandable during a down market when most stock prices are decreasing which is when you margin account will most likely be affected.

The affect will be a decrease in equity percentage. If your equity percentage decreases to twenty five percent or less, you will have only twenty four hours in which to bring in additional funds to your margin account or if possible additional stock eligible for margin you can deposit the shares to your account.

The intent is to deposit additional equity to your margin account. One more option available is to start liquidating (selling the stock on your margin account) in order to increase the equity percentage.

If you fail to meet the call, in the twenty-four hour period allotted, your brokerage company will be forced to liquidate enough of your stock to meet the maintenance call.

This is perfectly legal as it is most likely stated in the margin agreement you must sign before you start trading on margin. You should read your margin agreement carefully or have your stockbroker or attorney review it with you if you do not fully understand the terms of the agreement.

To avoid these types of situation and to keep a good rapport with their clients, most brokerage companies will increase the minimum equity percentage so that they can set a certain time limit in which their clients have to meet a HOUSE MAINTENANCE CALL, which can be anywhere from forty eight hours to five business days.

To better understand house maintenance calls let's continue using the sample margin account that we have already established. We were able to purchase additional shares of stock without depositing additional funds to the account.

Let's assume for example, five months after you have established your margin account that your investments have decreased in price per share dramatically due to an unstable market.

You receive a call from your stockbroker who informs you that you will be required to deposit additional funds to your margin account to cover a house maintenance call do to the fact that your margin account has fallen below the minimum equity percentage allowed by your brokerage company (in the example we will use thirty percent for the house minimum equity percentage allowed).

Your account reads as follows:

Jan. 15

Long: 200 ABC @17
           400 XYZ @3
Market Value: $4,600.00
Debit: $3,400.00
Equity: $1,200.00
Equity %: 26%
Maint. Call: $180.00

Keep in mind that we are using the house minimum equity percentage of thirty percent. In this example, the account equity percentage has fallen below the thirty percent minimum equity percentage allowed by the brokerage company and now reflects a house maintenance call.

To figure a margin account for house maintenance, we use this simple formula:

(Thirty Percent Of The Market Value, Minus the Equity)

.30 x $4,600.00 (M.V.) = $1,300.00
$1,380.00—$1,200.00 (Eq.) = $180.00 (Maint. Call)

At this point you will be required by your brokerage company to deposit one hundred and eighty dollars to your margin account. After depositing the required amount your account will read as follows:

Deposit: $ 180.00
Long: 200 ABC @17
           400 XYZ @3

Market Value: $4,600.00
Debit: $3,220.00
Equity: $1,380.00
Equity%:   30%

The account is now at thirty percent equity percentage, the minimum equity percentage allowed by this particular brokerage company. However, depositing cash to your margin account is not the only way to satisfy a maintenance call. If you have stock eligible for margin in your safe deposit box, you can deposit that stock to your margin account and apply its loan value towards the maintenance call or you could simply sell some or all of the stock already long on your margin account.

LIQUIDATING TO COVER MAINTENANCE CALLS

If you decide to liquidate (sell) some of your stock in order to satisfy a maintenance call, you must liquidate three and a third times the amount of the maintenance call.

You cannot sell a fraction of a share of stock and this leaves you with no choice but to liquidate to the nearest dollar amount of the maintenance call.

Going back to our example when the margin account had a house maintenance call of one hundred and eighty dollars, this time we will satisfy the call by liquidating two hundred shares of XYZ stock at three dollars per share. The account will read as follows:

Jan. 15

Sold: 200 XYZ @3
Long: 200*ABC @17*
            200 XYZ @3
Market Value: $4,000.00
Debit: $2,800.00
Equity: $1,200.00
Equity %:   30%

Your margin account is now thirty percent of the minimum equity percentage required by your brokerage company. It is in good practice to maintain your equity percentage above the minimum equity percent required because stock prices fluctuate throughout the business day and you can find your margin account below the minimum equity percentage allowed the very next day, even after satisfying a maintenance call.

Keep in mind that the thirty percent minimum equity percentage requirement is designed to alert you to the fact that your margin accounts equity percentage is declining close to the mandatory twenty-five or thirty percent minimum requirement that must be strictly enforced by all brokerage companies.

If your investments decline dramatically and your equity percentage falls below the twenty five or thirty percent minimum percentage allowed, then you will be required to satisfy that call within the next forty eight hours.

If you decide to liquidate some of your stock in order to satisfy your maintenance call under twenty-five or thirty percent, you will be required to liquidate four times the amount of the call.

To help you avoid maintenance calls, you should check the current prices of the stocks you have long on your margin account on a regular basis. If you notice that a specific stock or number of stocks are long on your margin account and are declining in price per share, you should contact your stockbroker as soon as possible and have him or her give you an update on your equity percentage and make your stockbroker aware of the declining prices of your investments.

Your stockbroker should be able to explain to you the possible reason for the declining stock prices and advise you on liquidating some of your investments to avoid further loss of your accounts equity or to hold on to your investments foreseeing a future increase in price per share of your investments, risking the possibility of your margin account falling below your brokerage company's minimum equity percentage allowed.

In such situations, your judgment should play a roll in this kind of decision-making. After all it is your money and it will be your loss if your stockbroker miscalculates his or her hunch.

REFIGURING YOUR MARGIN ACCOUNT

The practice of refiguring your margin account for the current equity percentage is a practice that every stock investor should take seriously.

Unfortunately, to many stock investors lose their investments to maintenance calls that could have been prevented if they had refigured their margin accounts for equity percentage on a regular basis.

The main reason why a lot of stock investors lose their investments to maintenance calls is because they are not notified of the declining price per share of their investments until their margin accounts have already fallen below the minimum equity percentage allowed by their brokerage companies.

This is similar to the little red light on your cars dashboard that blinks when your cars engine is low on oil.

If a service station is nowhere to be found, then you will have to pull your car off the road to avoid damage to your cars engine until you can get help.

Situations like this are an inconvenience and can be costly. For instance, towing fees or damage to your cars engine due to the loss of oil, but situations such as this can be avoided if you were to check your oil level in your cars engine on a regular basis such as every time you stop for gas.

If you find that your cars oil level is down a quart, you would simply add a quart of oil to your cars engine and if it happens on a regular basis you would bring your car to a service station and have the problem repaired.

The same theory holds true for maintaining the equity percentage on a margin account. If you check the equity percentage on a regular basis you will be able to save yourself from taking unforeseen losses to your investments.

By refiguring your margin account for equity percentage on a regular basis you will give yourself the advantage of getting out of certain investments before they become major losses to your portfolio.

You may feel that it is your stock brokers responsibility to monitor your margin account for declining stock prices, but lets face it, your stockbroker earns his or her living trying to solicit stock investments to as many clients and potential clients as possible and has very little time to focus his or her attention on your personal investments. However, this is not to say that your broker does not care what happens to your investments once he or she makes a commission on a sale.

It is up to you to keep an eye on your investments and work with your stockbroker to ensure that you profit from your investments and are able to avoid any major lose to your margin account.

Refiguring your margin account also gives you an advantage in an up market when your investments are doing well.

You will have the advantage of refiguring your account for excess equity and buying power. This will enable you to purchase more stock using your buying power to increase your potential profits.

If you already have an established margin account and would like to refigure it for equity percentage and possible buying power, just follow the example we will use to refigure a margin account for margin excess, buying power, equity percentage and possible maintenance call.

The first step is to get a copy of the most recent monthly financial statement that your brokerage company has provided to you.

Make a list of all the stocks long on your margin account. Next check the newspapers financial section for yesterday's closing prices, and then list the closing prices next to each of the stocks on your list that the price obtains to.

Your list should look similar to the list in the following example.

LONG	PRICE	MARKET VALUE
200 ABC	@12	$2,400.00
50 XYZ	@10 3/8	$ 518.75
100 EFG	@7	700.00
100 UVW	@5 ½	$ 550.00
		$4,168.75
		(CURRENT MARKET VALUE)

Now list the debit balance, which appears on your monthly financial statement, and subtract it from the current market value figure to arrive at your margin accounts current equity.

$1,500.00 (Debit Balance)

$4,168.75 (Current Market Value)
-$1,500.00 (Debit Balance)
_____
$2,668.75 (Equity)

Now you can refigure your margin account for the current margin excess and buying power.

Divide your current market value by fifty percent and subtract that figure from your current equity figure to arrive at the current margin excess.

$4,168.75 (Current Market Value)
x   .50
_____
$2,084.37

$2,668.75 (Current Equity)
$2,084.37 50% of Current Market Value)
_____
$ 584.38 (Margin Excess)

Now multiply the margin excess by two, to arrive at your current buying power.

$ 584.38
x 2
_____

$1,168.76 (Current Buying Power)

You should contact your stockbroker and compare your figures with your stockbroker's current figures of your margin account.

If your figures do not coincide with your stockbroker's figures, ask him or her how they arrived at conflicting figures.

Keep in mind that your figures are only an estimate because your margin account may have been charged monthly interest on the debit it carries since you've received your latest monthly financial statement. Also, the price per share of your stocks may have increased or decreased from the time you refigured your margin account until the time you actually contacted your stockbroker.

SELLING SHORT ON MARGIN

Selling short on margin is basically the opposite theory of buying stock long on margin. Instead of buying stock and anticipating the price per share to increase, you can sell stock that you do not own in anticipation that the price per share of that stock will decrease.

Once the price per share of the stock, which you sold short on margin decreases, you can buy it back at its now lower price per share and gain a profit.

The first question that most investors ask is, how can I sell stock that I do not own? The answer to that question is somewhat obvious. Whenever you want to use something that you do not own you would seek to borrow it.

If you intend to sell stock that you do not own, your stockbroker can inquire about borrowing the shares for you from your brokerage company. If your brokerage company does not have the shares available they will inquire about borrowing the shares from another brokerage firm. Be assured, there will be a fee charged to you for these efforts.

Once your stockbroker has obtained the shares of stock you have requested to sell short, a sell order will be placed. When the sell order goes through your margin account will reflect a short position (the amount of shares you have sold short) with a minus market value, a credit and a margin call.

To simplify all of this, the following example will demonstrate how a margin account reads after a short sale.

Example:

Aug. 1   Sold: 100 XYZ @40

Short: 100 XYZ @40
Short M.V.: $4,000.00
Credit: $4,000.00
Equity: -0-
Margin Call: $2,000.00

Notice that the margin account has a credit but no equity. This is due to the minus market value resulting from the sale of stock which you do not own which means you are not entitled to the proceeds of the sale.

The margin account also reflects a margin call. Margin calls are calculated at fifty percent requirement of the sale. In the example one hundred shares of stock were sold at forty dollars per share of stock were sold at forty dollars per share for a total sale value of four thousand dollars. The required deposit will be two thousand dollars.

(.5 x $4,000.00 = $2,000.00)

Most brokerage companies have a minimum price per share requirement for margin accounts. For example, your brokerage company may require that your margin call be calculated at five dollars per share on stock that is priced under their minimum price per share requirement. This minimum price per share requirement usually ranges between three to five dollars per share.

There is also the minimum equity requirement of two thousand dollars. These requirements make it important to know just how much it will cost you to sell short before you place any orders.

To get back to the example, lets see how the margin account reads after depositing the required fifty percent of the sale value.

Aug. 7

Deposit: $2,000.00
Short: 100 XYZ @40
Short Market Value: $4,000.00
Credit: $6,000.00
Equity: $2,000.00
Equity %: 50%

To arrive at the equity, subtract the short market value from the credit.

($4,000.00 Market Value—$6,000.00 Credit = $2,000.00 Equity)

To arrive at the equity percentage, divide the equity by the short Market value.

($2,000 EQ. + $4,000 S.M.V. = .5 or 50%)

Selling short on margin seem very confusing at times but, heep in mind that selling short has similar requirements when compared to buying stock long on margin. It's almost as if you're trading in a reverse fashion.

PROFITING FROM SHORT SALES

As already determined, the purpose for selling stock short is to buy it back at a lower price than the original sale price. To better understand this; Let's continue with the example of a short sale of stock at forty-five dollars per share:

Aug. 16th

Short: 100 XYZ @31
S.M.V. $3,100
Credit: $6,000
Equity: $2,900
Equity %:   93%

Now let's assume that you decided to buy back the one hundred shares of XYZ stock at thirty one dollars per share, your account will read as follows:

Aug. 16th

Bought: 100 XYZ @31
Credit: $2,900
Profit: $900

After buying back the stock you sold short at a price per share less than that of the sale price, your account will reflect a credit consisting of the two thousand dollars you deposited to meet the initial margin call and the difference you deposited to meet the price of the short sale and the buy back.

The difference between the price of the short sale and the buy back was nine hundred dollars. The following example will show how we arrive at this figure:

Sold: 100 XYZ @40 = $4,000 Credit

Bought: 100 XYZ @31 = $3,100 Debit

Profit: $900 Credit

When you sold the shares short you created a credit balance (not considered a FREE CREDIT balance) that you are not entitled to due to the fact that you do not own the stock that you sold. But, if the price per share decreases and you buy the shares back you will be entitled to the remaining credit balance that is considered your profit.

WHEN TO SELL SHORT

There can be a number of reasons for selling stock short. One general reason why an investor would sell stock short is due to a negative news report concerning a certain company.

Companies reporting financially troubled times usually will find the price per share of their stock starting to decrease almost immediately. The decrease in the price per share of the company's stock is the direct result of it's shareholders bailing out of their investments in order to minimize any losses.

Another reason for declining stock prices is simply a down market. Most stock investors see an up market as the only way to profit by investing in stock and a down market as only a definite way to lose money. But, given the opportunity to sell short in a down market (such as during a crash or correction) can net you some hefty profits.

Some stock analyst predict down markets in advance which can actually be the cause of a down market as it will have stock investors scrambling to sell certain stocks in order to minimize loses that can be sustained in a down market. On the other hand, some investors may be taking advantage of a bailout during a down market by selling short in order to profit from this type of chaos.

One good example of this may be the crash of the market on October 19, 1987. This crash obviously caused many stock investors to panic and start to dump their investments in order to minimize losses. In addition to individual investors dumping their shares was the large institutions such as brokerage houses and banks that had their computers programmed to start selling off stocks in volume when the stocks they were holding hit specified (low) prices per share.

This combination of selling led to a virtual melt down effect of the market, which in turn led to future changes known as fail safe systems such as halting trading when selling volumes hit a specified number set forth by officials in charge of the market.

Getting back to selling short, in drastically down markets, you are almost guaranteed to profit from selling short. But, in reality we can't sit around a quote machine waiting for a down market to strike in order to sell short. You can always sell a certain stock short and wait for the results (profit or lose) hoping you profit from a declining price per share of that particular stock and hope you don't kick yourself for not purchasing the stock long on margin instead.

There is a way to hedge against this from happening to you; it's called 'Short versus the Box'.

SHORT VS. BOX

To hedge against a loss by selling a particular stock short would be to buy that same stock long on the margin account.

Example:

Buy: 100 XYZ @45

Sell Short: 100 XYZ @45

Your Margin Account Reads:

Long: 100 XYZ @45
Short: 100 XYZ @45

Fed Call: $ 450

Notice that you have created a Fed Call of $450 (or $2,000 if you do not have the $2,000 minimum equity requirement satisfied in your margin account) this is due to a requirement of ten per cent margin on initial Short vs. the Box trades.

If you were to close out either the long buy or the short sale (this is known as lifting a leg) you would be required to put up an additional forty percent in order to meet the margin requirements as if you were to buy long or sell short *only*.

Yet there is still another way to hedge against potential loss when anticipating selling or buying a stock for profit, it's known as *STOCK OPTIONS*.

Stock Options

STOCK OPTIONS

Stock options are contracts to Buy or Sell certain stocks at specified prices. These contracts have expiration dates ranging anywhere from thirty days to one year. The expiration date and the stocks versatility determine the price of each stock option contract.

The price of the stock option is in technical terms known as the *PREMIUM* and, premiums for stock options generally range from two hundred dollars to six hundred dollars.

Stock options to buy or sell certain stocks at specified prices are technically know as *CALL* and *PUT* options.

CALL OPTIONS: The right to purchase a certain stock at a specified price on or before the expiration date.

PUT OPTIONS: The right to sell a certain stock at a specified price on or before expiration date.

STRIKE PRICE: The specified price is known as the *STRIKE PRICE.*

CONTRACT: For every one CALL or Put purchased you are technically purchasing One

CONTRACT. For each contract purchased, you will be entitled to exercise the purchase or sale of one hundred shares of a particular stock.

To simplify and better understand stock options, let's see how a cash account will read after purchasing a call option.

Let's assume that you were to purchase one Call of ABC stock options at two hundred and fifty dollars pre contract with a Strike Price of forty-five dollars. Your cash account will read as follows:

Purchased: 1 CALL ABC Dec. 3 @45
Debit: $250
Equity: —0—
Market Value: -0-

After you have deposited funds to cover the Premium of the stock option CALL, your cash account will only reflect the fact that you have purchased a CALL option. In most cases, your cash account will not reflect any market value or equity such as it does when purchasing stock. This is not to say that your purchase of a CALL option is worthless when in fact you can actually sell your CALL option if you chose to.

The reason no market value or equity is reflected is due to the fact that CALL and PUT options alike have an expiration date which render CALLS and PUTS as worthless if they were to expire without ever being exercised or sold.

After the purchase your cash account will read:

Long: 1 CALL ABC DEC. 3 @45

Or

1 (number of contracts purchased)
CALL (the option to *buy* a certain stock)
ABC (name of stock that you have the option to buy)
DEC. 3 (date option expires)
@45 (strike price)

If you were to purchase a Put option instead, all the same principles would apply except the fact that you will have the option to sell a certain stock at a specified price. Using the same example as the purchase of a Call option, your cash account will read as follows:

Long: 1 PUT ABC Dec. 3 @45

Or

1 (number of contracts purchased)
CALL (the option to *Sell* a certain stock)
ABC (name of stock that you have the option to sell)
DEC. 3 (date option expires)
@45 (strike price)

As discussed previously in selling short on margin–lets see what alternative roll the Put stock option plays in a down market.

PUT OPTIONS

Let's assume that ABC stock is selling at forty-five dollars per share. News of corporate corruption and scandal has been released to the public and lawsuits against the company are starting to multiply. Or let's say for example that the market is taking a tumble and is taking a toll on ABC stock.

The investors of ABC stock are starting to bail out of their investment in order to minimize their loses as the price per share of ABC stock is starting to decrease due to the recently released news or the down market.

With no foreseeable chance of recovery at the present time, you could sell short some of the ABC stock. But, that would require at least two thousand dollars to be tied up in order to meet the minimum equity requirement on an initial short sale on margin. Unless you have enough equity in an existing margin account to cover such a sale.

PUT options, as a cheaper alternative to selling short would be the way to go when trying to profit on a declining stock.

The next example will examine how you can profit from purchasing a Put option against a stock declining in price per share.

September: 5 ABC stock selling at forty-five dollars per share

CASH ACCOUNT READS:

Purchase: 1 PUT ABC Dec. 3 @45

Debit: $250

Most brokerage companies require that your cash account have sufficient cash available when purchasing stock options. Assuming that your account has sufficient cash available you now own One Contract to sell one hundred share of ABC company stock at forty-five dollars per share.

After short period of time, the ABC stock is now selling at thirty-five dollars per share. A ten-dollar per share drop since you've purchased the Put stock option with a Strike Price of forty-five dollars per share.

At this point you may want to exercise your Put option for a profit. If you decide to exercise your Put stock option, your account will read as follows:

September 15th—ABC stock selling at thirty five dollars per share

CASH ACCOUNT READS:

Exercise: 1 PUT ABC Dec. 3 @45

Credit Balance: $4,500

Short: 100 ABC @35 (current market price)

Buy back: 100 ABC @35 (current market price) $3,500

Profit: $1,000 minus the price of the PUT

Of course, if you had 100 ABC stock long on your account at the time of the stock option exercise, there would be no need flatten the exercise with a buy back. If would be a clean wash.

CALL OPTIONS

Call options are traded with the intention of profiting from stocks increasing in value as opposed to Put stock options, which are traded with the intention of profiting from stocks decreasing in value. For example, let's assume, under different circumstances, that ABC stock is currently selling at forty five dollars per share and has just released it's quarterly report to it's shareholders. The quarterly report reflects a profit and an increase in the company's capital.

This in itself will cause the price per share of ABC stock to increase, but let's assume that ABC company has just released news that it has won a contract to manufacture and supply parts to a major builder of airplanes.

When companies release news of this magnitude, the price per share of that company's stock is sure to skyrocket due to the increase in volume of shares being purchased by stock investors who want to profit from that company's good fortune.

But what if a company releases a statement stating only the possibilities of such a contract exist and no agreements have been finalized. This means that there is nothing definite about the news they have just released but such a statement made to the public will have speculative stock investors jumping at the chance to get in on the ground floor of a potentially profitable stock.

There is a risk however that you could end up taking a loss by investing in stock based merely on speculation. The fact that the news released by the company is not of definitive nature will cause the price per share of that company 's stock to rapidly decrease once news of that company's failure to obtain the contract that was to be that company's bread and butter is mad public.

Situations such as this can be very frustrating to a stock investor. He or she will feel that investing in a certain stock based on speculation is to risky and at the same time feel anxiety to purchase as many shares as possible just in case that company makes good on its quest to close on a deal that its share holders will profit from.

Call Options can alleviate the frustrations that go along with the decision whether or not to invest in stock based on speculation. More important, call options will reduce the risk of losing bundle of money on an investment that does not live up to its expectations.

The following examples will demonstrate how call options will reduce the risk of investing in stock based on speculation and how you can profit from a stock that lives up to it's expectations and invest less money than it would cost you if you were to purchase the actual shares of that stock.

Let's assume that ABC stock is currently trading at forty-five dollars per share and speculative reports were made about the company's future plans and, business dealings that spell nothing but future profits for anyone holding shares of this company's stock.

Let's also assume that you decided to purchase one hundred shares of ABC stock at forty five dollars per share with the anticipation that ABC stock will increase in price per share as soon as the company succeeds in accomplishing it's goals.

Sept. 1ˢᵗ

Bought: 100 ABC @45

Long: 100 ABC @45
M.V. $4,500
Debit: $4,500
Equity: -0-

Now that you've purchased one hundred shares of ABC stock, you must deposit to your Cash account forty five hundred dollars. At this point, you are also risking the whole forty five hundred dollars due to the fact that you bought the stock based on speculation.

To demonstrate the risk involved, let's follow the fluctuating price per share of the ABC stock.

After paying for your purchase of ABC stock, you notice that the price per share has increased. This could be attributed to the fact that there are other speculative stock investors out there who may also be investing in ABC stock or ABC stock may be starting to move up as expected. This upward movement in the price per share will have you monitoring this stocks price regularly.

Sept. 8ᵗʰ

Deposit: $4,500

Long: 100 ABC @50
M.V. $5,000
Equity: $5,000

You may very well be satisfied with a gain of five hundred dollars but, with the speculation that this stock may increase another five points or more, you stand to make at least another five hundred dollars additional profit.

This is the risk and frustration of investing in stock because the price per share could decrease slowly or instantly losing your entire gain.

Sept. 15th

Long:	100 ABC @45
M.V.:	$4,500
Equity:	$4,500

The price per share has just dropped back to the original price per share at which you first purchased the stock.

Sept. 22nd

Long:	100 ABC @44
M.V.:	$4,400
Equity:	$4,400

After one week the ABC stock has dropped below the original purchase price that means you are now holding stock at a loss of five hundred dollars.

To avoid such a situation, you could have invested in *CALL* stock options. A Call stock option could give a stock investor a low risk opportunity to either profit from a stock that measures up to it's expectations without depositing forty five hundred dollars to his or her cash account or, a minimize the stock investors loss by the cost of the Call stock option itself.

The following examples will demonstrate how Call stock options work for each of these situations.

Sept. 1st

Current price per share of ABC stock: $45

Bought:	100 ABC @45
Long:	100 ABC @45
M.V.:	$4,500
Debit:	$4,500

If you were to purchase a *CALL* stock option instead, your cash account would read as follows:

Sept. 1st

Current price of Call stock option for ABC stock @45 is: $250

Bought:	1 Call ABC Dec. 1 @45
Debit:	$250

Obviously there is a big difference between the purchase prices of the stock versus the purchase price of the Call stock option.

At this point you may be wondering why you would bother to buy stock long on your cash account or sell it short on margin if you could easily trade stock options. The answer is simple: TIME.

Time is a major factor in the stock investment game. PUT and Call stock options have expiration dates while the purchase or short sale of stock has no chronological time limit enabling to buy and or sell at your discretion.

Now let's get back to how to profit from Call stock options using the same example:

Sept. 1st

Current price per share of ABC stock: $45

Bought: 1 Call ABC Dec.1 @45 (current value $250)

Let's assume that over a four-week period after you've purchased your Call stock options that ABC stock has increased in price per share to fifty-five dollars. At this time you may consider exercising your Call stock option to take advantage of this increase.

Your account will read as follows:

Oct. 1st

Exercise:1 Call ABC Dec. 1 @45
Buy: 100 ABC @45
Long:100 ABC @45
Debit: $4,500

After the Call stock option exercise takes place you will want to sell the ABC stock at the current market price.

Sell: 100 ABC @55
Credit: $1,000

Your account now reflects a credit balance of one thousand dollars, a $750 dollar profit after you consider the two hundred and fifty dollars you had to pay to purchase the Call stock option.

This is how you can profit from stock options without risking thousands of dollars hoping that the stock you purchased will increase in value in a short amount of time.

DECIMALIZATION

(Special Addition to Stock Investors Technology Manual)

On August 28, 2000, the investment industry initiated Phase One of trading stocks in dollars and cents, instead of fractions, which has been the tradition since trading first began. Phase One of "decimalization" consists of twelve companies on the New York Stock Exchange and American Stock Exchange already trading dollars and cents.

Decimalization will keep the American markets competitive with the foreign markets abroad, which already trade stock in decimals (dollars and cents American). Phase Two of Decimalization scheduled for September 25, 2000 includes from fifty to one hundred listed stocks (along with their associated Stock Options).

Although full implementation is slated for April 9,2001, an evaluation of Decimalization and it's impact on the investment world will take place to determine if a full conversion of all listed securities and their stock options is a go.

In early march of 2001, a limited number of Nasdaq issues and their associated options will be converted to decimals. After early April of 2001, a full implementation of all Markets combined will be scheduled to go into effect.

Until the full implementation of Decimalization has taken effect, it will still be of importance to you as a stock investor to calculate and refigure your stock portfolio using fractions and to use the fractions to decimal conversion system and chart provided in Stock Investors Terminology Manual.

Other Ways To Profit

DIRECT INVESTMENT PLANS

Many large corporations offer Direct Purchase Plans, which allow stock investors to purchase shares of stock directly from corporations without having to pay any commission charges.

As we all know, nothing in this world is free, although there is no commission charges on Direct Investment Plans (because there is no Stock-broker involved) there most likely will be an application fee especially if you choose to invest in a company the offers an annual purchase plan.

The way an annual purchase plan works is that you decide how much you would like to invest into the Direct Investment Plan. The dollar amounts that you can choose will vary and cane as low as one hundred dollars.

The purpose of investing in a Direct Investment Plan is to purchase as many shares as possible with the dollar amount you have allotted to the plan. In other words, if the price of the stock that you choose to invest in drops, then you will be able to purchase more shares than could when that particular stock is selling at it's peak.

Another advantage to Direct Investment Plans is that you will be able to purchase fractional shares of a particular company's stock. The fractional shares subsequently add up to up to whole shares after time.

The only real drawback to investing in Direct Investment Plans is that you can't sell your shares immediately as you could if your trading on-line or with a stockbroker because you have to submit your order to sell in writing.

DIVIDEND REINVESTMENT PLANS

Another way to invest directly in a particular company's stock is to choose a stock that offers dividend reinvestments. Dividend reinvestments allow a stock investor to invest in additional shares a particular company's stock using the dividends paid to the stock investor on record.

Usually the shares will be purchased at a discount allowing the stock investor to purchase more shares than would be allowed at the current market price per share coupled with the additional savings of having to pay no commission fees as there is no stockbroker involve in these transactions.

OTHER WAYS TO COLLECT DIVIDENDS

You don't have to drive yourself crazy looking for stocks that offer dividend reinvestment plans in order to profit from dividends. Most Blue Chip companies offer their investors cash dividends, although they may not be dividend reinvestment plans with discounts, you will still profit from them.

Still another way to invest in stocks that pay dividends is to consider investing in

Preferred stock. Preferred stock investors receive dividends before the holders of that particular company's common stock.

Or, as discussed earlier in this you can and should consider investing in Income Stocks.

Income Stocks are usually utilities such as gas or electric companies that pay out dividends on a quarterly basis. The only drawback to Income Stocks is that the price per share usually remains constant. This means that most of your profits will be made on the dividends that they pay out.

Restrictions

What You Can't Do!

There are many rules and regulations that govern stock investing. Many stock

Investors are not aware of these rules and regulations and often make the same common mistakes when it comes to opening a stock portfolio or stock account and just start trading.

The most common mistake made by stock investors is known as the Liquidation. The Liquidation is the practice of liquidating (selling one security in order to cover the purchase of another security on two different days.

In other words, if you already have an established cash account and have stock long on your cash account that is fully paid for and you decide to purchase additional shares of stock and plan on selling one of the stocks long in your cash account to cover the cost of the new purchase, you must execute each trade on the same day.

Executing the Buy side and the Sell side on the same day is known as a Same Day Substitution. The purpose of the Same Day Substitution is to sell enough stock in order to cover the entire or a portion of the purchase (if your intension is to cover a portion of the purchase price through a Liquidation, you must pay off the remainder in cash).

This type of trading is permitted and in no way discouraged (especially since your paying a commission on both sides of the trades).

If on the other hand, you've decided to sell a stock in order to cover the purchase of another stock on two separate days, you will be incurring what is known as a Liquidation.

The following is an example of both types of trading:

Same Day Substitution:

Aug. 1st

Purchase: 100 ABC @40
Sell: 200 XYZ @20

Balance: -0-

Liquidation:

Aug. 1st

Purchase: 100 ABC @40

Balance: $4,000

Aug. 2nd

Sell: 200 XYZ @20
Balance: -0-

Liquidating is frowned upon and a record of how many times you trade in this manner is kept for a twelve-month period. Within this twelve month period, you will be able to liquidate up to tree times before your account is restricted to "Ninety Days/Cash On Hand Trading Only'.

This means that for the next ninety days, you will be required to have cash on hand in your cash account to cover the purchase of any new trades on trade date.

Day Trading In The Cash Account

Buying a specific stock in the cash account and selling that same stock on the same day without depositing any funds or having any funds on hand to cover the purchase is known as a Day Trade and will get your account restricted to a 'Ninety Day Restriction/Cash On Hand Trading Only'. Day Trading in the cash account without any funds on hand to cover the full amount of the purchase is not tolerated. Some brokerage

Companies may lift the restriction if you deposit the funds by settlement date to cover your commitment, or you may very well be asked to close your account and go somewhere else and trade.

Another way to get your cash account restricted to 'Ninety Days /Cash On Hand Only' trading is to purchase a specific stock on one day and selling the same stock on another day. This may not be a Same Day Substitution but the penalty is the same. Also, like the Day Trade, if you deposit the funds into your cash account by settlement date, the restriction will be lifted.

This type of trading is tolerated a little more than Day Trading in the cash account because sometimes you must bail out of a trade as soon as possible in order to curtail a major loss if the bottom falls out of the stock you just purchased or, you may have to sell your purchase immediately in order to secure a significant profit.

These types of situations are understandable and most likely to be overlooked as long as the original commitment is met by trade date.

The following examples will show losing trades and winning trades that may move you to sell your stock immediately (regardless of the rules and regulations).

Losing Trade:

Aug 5th

Purchase: 100 ABC @40

_____

Aug 6th

Sell: 100 ABC @30

Loss: $1,000

The loss to this cash account could have been greater if the investor waited until settlement date to sell.

Winning Trade:

Aug 5th

Purchase: 100 ABC @40

_____

Aug 6th

Sell: 100 ABC @50

Profit: $1,000

In order to secure a profit, you may have to sell your original purchase before settlement date but, make sure (the same goes for the losing situation) that you meet the original commitment by settlement date.

HEY, THAT'S NOT FAIR!

At this point you may be thinking that it is unfair of the brokerage company that you do business with to punish you so harshly and swiftly because you feel that you have until settlement date to meet your commitments and that being that, you feel that you should have until settlement date before ant penalties are imposed on your account.

So why *do* brokerage companies place cash accounts on 'Ninety Day/Cash On Hand Only' restrictions immediately if there's a chance that you will meet your commitment on a timely basis?

The reasoning behind this seemingly harsh penalty is that a large population of stock investors will not bother to deposit the funds needed to meet their commitments (purchases) and, charging a restriction to the cash account immediately helps the brokerage company keep more accurate books.

It is important for your brokerage company to keep accurate records of Day Trades and Liquidations because when they (brokerage companies) are audited by the exchange, they are penalized for inaccurate or missed Day Trades (in the cash account) and/or Liquidations.

So if you want to keep in good standings with your brokerage company, it is important to meet all of your commitments on a timely basis.

MORE RESTRICTIONS

Stock brokerage companies, whether they place trades for you On-line or with a traditional stockbroker or financial adviser or planner, must adhere to a variety of rules and regulations the same as you, the stock investor (client).Here are some other ways you may end up with a restricted cash account.

As mentioned, always meet your commitments on a timely basis if possible, but we all know that nobody is perfect and that is why Extensions of time are granted.

Extensions of time are granted to cash account trades when funds for a stock purchase have not arrived in the cash account on time. Keep in mind that Extensions of time do not apply to cash account Day Trades or Liquidations; payments to satisfy these particular situations must be deposited by settlement date of the purchase.

The most popular reason (excuse) given for funds not received to cover a trade on time is the old 'Check Is In The Mail'routine. If your funds are still not received by the time your Extension of time has expired (which is five business days), the brokerage company you do business with has the right to (and responsibility to) sell your purchase at the market (current price per share) to meet and satisfy your commitment.

Guess what? Your cash account will immediately be placed on a 'Ninety Day/Cash On Hand Trading Only' restriction. Make note that this rule also applies to Fed Calls in the margin account as well.

Keep in mind that any loses incurred in your cash account due to a sellout at the current market price per share will be your losses (you have to make up the lose).

The following example shows how such losses are incurred:

Sept. 4th

Purchase: 200 EFG @50

Debit: $10,000

_____

Sept. 9th

Extension: Applied

Market Value: 200 EFG @45 = $9,000

Debit: $10,000

_____

Sept. 16th

Sell Out: 200 EFG @40 = $8,000

Debit: (Loss) $2,000

Loss incurred is $2,000

Selling out the trade sooner should have minimized the loss incurred in the above example. This is not the fault of the brokerage company because they had no right to sellout the account any sooner than they did but, the fault of the client and the stock broker who just watched the bottom fall out of this particular stock.

Monthly Financial Statements

Reading your monthly financial statement provided to you by your stock brokerage company that you do business with, may at time seem as though you are deciphering a coded message when trying to balance your stock portfolio.

Competing stock brokerage companies use different formats when producing monthly financial statements for their clients. But, all draw one conclusion they all try to consolidate.

Consolidating the format of the monthly financial statement is cost efficient and provides for a better understanding of the past thirty days of activity that has taken place in your account because separate pages are not necessary to describe and interpret the various form of entries that can take place in your account over a thirty day period.

Understanding your brokerage company's monthly financial statement may seem a little difficult but, by using a simple method of breaking down the activity recorded on your monthly financial statement you will better understand what has taken place in your account and help you to interpret your monthly financial statement and eventually understand what has taken place in your account over the past thirty days simple by scanning through your monthly financial statement and pausing only on any entries that require careful examination.

The method of breaking down the activity on your monthly financial statement is to divide your monthly financial statement into three separate columns. Each column will play multiple rolls. For example, Column *A* will describe the number of shares withdrawn from your account either by sale, delivery or journal entry.

Column *B* on the other hand will describe the number of shares deposited to your account either by purchase, receipt of shares or journal entry.

The third column, Column *C* is reserved for the description of the entries made to your account. Descriptions include the names of the securities being purchased or sold in your account, identify journal entries and funds deposited or paid out of your account.

To get a clearer understanding of theses three columns and how each function separately and in unison, let's begin by demonstrating each columns function and why it is necessary to have separate columns perform multiple functions.

Column *A* will depict stock being purchased in a stock portfolio and stock also being received into a stock portfolio.

Column *B* will depict stock being sold from a stock portfolio and also stock being delivered off of a stock portfolio.

Example 1a:

Monthly Financial Statement

	A		C
Purchase:	100		XYZ Co. @10
Received:	200		ABC Co. @16

Example 1b:

Monthly Financial Statement

	B		C
Sold:	100		EFG Co. @10
Delivered:	200		UVW Co. @5

At this point both columns appear to be identical barring the entry memos (purchase, receive, sold and delivered) and bare no reason for having a column *A* or a column *B*. But, as suggested, consolidating the format of the monthly financial statement will permit each column to perform multiple (different) functions.

By aligning column *A* alongside column *B* you will have a better understanding for the need of more than one column to account for the activity in your account over the past month.

Example 2:

Monthly Financial Statement

	A	B	C
Purchase:	100		XYZ Co. @10
Sold:		100	EFG Co. @10
Received:	200		ABC Co. @16
Delivered:	200		UVW Co. @5

At a glance you should be able to determine when stock if stock is coming into your account or going out of your account either by purchase or deposit (receive), or by sale or delivery.

To simplify the reading of your monthly financial statement even more, let's look at column *A* as the Plus (+) column and column *B* as the minus (-) column. This will help you to better understand your monthly financial statement as we now apply money to our example.

Example 2:

Monthly Financial Statement

	A (+)	B (-)	C Description
Purchased:	100		XYZ Co. @10
Funds	$1,000		Check Received
Sold	$1,200	100	XYZ *Co. @12*
Funds		$1,200	Check Paid

On the purchase of one hundred shares of XYZ Co. at ten dollars per share, column *A* (+) depicts one hundred shares of stock coming into the account and column *B* (-) depicts the total price per share of the purchase by debiting the account.

As funds are received into your account to pay for the purchase of stock, column *A* (+) depicts one thousand dollars being credited to the account.

On the sale of XYZ Co. at twelve dollars per share, column *A* (+) depicts the proceeds of the sale of stock as a credit to the account and column *B* (-) depicts one hundred shares of stock leaving the account.

As the proceeds of the sale are paid to the client, the B(-) depicts one thousand two hundred dollars being debited to the account.

The description column was informing you as to what each and every entry to the account represented. Such as the name of the stock purchased and sold and at which specific prices and number of shares. The description column also informed you about the debit and credit to the account, for example, the description of the debit was informing you that a check was paid out of the account and the description of the credit was informing you that a check was deposited to the account.

Using the terms A (+) to represent a plus (or positive) to the account and B (-) to represent a minus (or negative) to the account is to help the stock investor grasp a simple understanding of the functions that each of these columns play.

On a real monthly financial statement your brokerage company will more than likely the technical terms CREDIT/DEL which simple means credits and or deliveries of stock to the account and other short terms such as the following:

SOLD/CREDIT—stock sold in the account and funds credited to the account.

BOUGHT /DEBIT–stock bought in the account and funds debited to the account.

The use of technical terms used among different stockbroker companies may vary and confuse you if you do business with more than one brokerage company. But, no matter what technical terms are used, you'll find that they all basically represent A (+) and B (-).

Journals

JOURNALS BETWEEN ACCOUNTS

The word journal describes the intentional movement of cash or stock on your account by means other than by purchase or sale of stock or, funds being deposited into or withdraws by check.

For example, you may have more than one account with the brokerage company that you do business with. Perhaps a husband and wife have a joint account and each also holds a single individual account.

Let's assume that this is the situation and the wife has decided to purchase one hundred shares of ABC Co. stock at ten dollars per share in her single individual account but does not have enough funds available in the particular account to cover the trade.

Wife's' account reads:

	A (+)	B (-)	Description
Feb 1st:			
Purchase:	100	$1,000	ABC C0.

Now let's assume that her husband has agreed to let his wife journal one thousand dollars from their joint account to her single individual account on settlement date of her purchase.

Just in case you are wondering, this is not a sexist statement to say that the husband allowed the wife to use one thousand dollars from their joint account. There are legalities involved when movement is made in joint accounts no matter who the joint recipients are.

No matter what the joint situation is, husband and wife, business partner, two brothers, two sisters a brother and sister and so on, when one party of the joint account wants to withdraw funds or securities from the joint account for whatever reason, the second party of the joint account must sign a letter authorizing the party of the first part to proceed with the withdrawal.

The letter know technically as an LOA (Letter Of Authority), must specify the exact dollar amount to be withdrawn from the joint account and the exact number of securities to be withdrawn from the joint account, which ever the situation if not both.

The letter or LOA must also specify where the funds and or securities are to be deposited to, such as another account within the brokerage company at hand.

In our example, the LOA is a binding legal agreement between the husband and wife. Once the one thousand dollar journal is made between the two accounts, the husband cannot rescind the LOA.

If a journal is being made from a single individual account to a joint account, than an LOA would not be necessary, just an OK from the client to the brokerage company or stockbroker to go ahead and make the journal.

An LOA does not have to be a formally written letter from your attorney, just a neat legible letter clearly explaining your intentions. You can use the following example LOA as a guide to writing your own LOA if ever needed.

Keep in mind that the example LOA being used is a continuation of the example being used to show how a husband and wife journal funds between their joint account to the wife's single individual account.

Sample LOA

To Whom It May Concern

Please use this Letter Of Authorization to journal one thousand dollars from our joint account #00000001 to my single individual account #0000002 to cover the purchase of one hundred shares of ABC stock at ten dollars per share.

Sincerely,

_____

Wife's signature
Husband's signature

After the LOA has been submitted to the stockbroker and the trade and the journal has been made the wife's monthly financial statement will read as follows:

Wife's account:

Monthly Financial Statement

	A (+)	B (-)	Description
Purchase:	100	$1,000	ABC C0. @10
Journal:	$1,000		jnl fm acct #0000001

The wife's single individual monthly financial statement now reflects the purchase of one hundred shares of ABC Co. stock at ten dollars per share requiring one thousand dollars to be deposited to this account to meet this commitment.

Her monthly financial statement also reflects the necessary funds being deposited in the form of a journal between this account on her joint account with her husband in order to meet her commitment.

JOURNALING STOCK

Stock can also be transferred between accounts as well as funds. Let's assume that the husband has sold one hundred shares of XYZ Co. not long on his single individual account but is long and is being held in safekeeping on his wife's single individual account.

Naturally the wife must sign an LOA in order to have the stock moved from her account to her husbands account (just her signature alone is required this time because she is the sole recipient of the account and owner of the stock long on the account). As mentioned, the stock is being held in safekeeping and cannot be released (journaled) until the wife signs a stock power and delivers it to her Brokerage Company or stockbroker.

Now let's further assume that an LOA was received by the stockbroker via the mail instructing him/her to execute the sale of one hundred shares of XYZ Co. at the market (current market price).

When the stockbroker checked wife's single individual account he realizes that the stock that is long and to be sold in the husbands single individual account is being held in safekeeping, he/she immediately mails a stock power to the wife to be signed so that he/she can get the stock released from safekeeping and back into negotiable form.

This will not delay the request that the stockbroker received to sell the shares at the market since he/she already holds the LOA to execute the trade and journal the shares between the two accounts to meet the commitment.

If the stockbroker decides to go ahead and execute the trade, he/she only has to worry about getting the signed stock power back from the wife by in time to meet the commitment on the sale.

The commitment I'm referring to is the sale of stock not long on the husbands account. After the trade is executed the husband's account will reflect a short position

(the shares that were sold) and an unsettled credit balance from the sale.

An unsettled credit balance means that the proceeds from the sale of stock even if the shares were available on trade date, are not available to the seller until the sale settles.

In certain situations an exception is made, such as for medical emergencies for example and the client will be charged a prepayment charge.

Bonus Section

TRADING BONDS

The reason for this special Trading Bonds section in a book specifi-cally targeting Stock Trading is that Bond Trading follows basic rules and regulations similar to Stock Trading and if can help you diversify your account without going out and buying another book about bond trading then more power to you.

Let's get started with a very popular and for the most part, Low Risk bond. The type of bond I'm referring to is a Municipal Bond. The Municipal Bond is commonly known as a Muni Bond.

The reason these bonds are referred to as Municipal Bonds or Muni Bonds (from here on out) is because they are issued by Government Agencies such as Sewer, Highways, Transportation Etc.

The advantage and popularity to purchasing a Muni Bond is that not only are they relatively safe, the interest paid out to investors is exempt from Federal Income Tax and, if you just happen to live in the same state as the bond issue you could also be exempt from local taxes as well.

Investing in a Muni Bond is very much like loaning government agencies money for a specified amount of time. The agency will in turn pay you interest on this so-called loan.

All Muni Bonds have a maturity date and that maturity date depends on the bond issue that you choose to invest in. Maturity dates can vary from a few moths to a few decades.

From the date of purchase to the date of maturity you will receive annual interest payments on specified dates and, on maturity date you will receive the full principle amount (face value of the bond).

MUNI BONDS AND CASH ACCOUNTS

Purchasing a Muni Bond in the cash account is very similar to purchasing stock in the cash account. But, yet they differ in various aspects

One way that Muni Bonds and Stocks simulate each other when purchased in the cash account is that you must pay one hundred percent of the purchase price, they both have a settlement date of three days where they differ is that Stock is eligible for an extension of time while Muni Bonds are exempt from extensions of time if you don't deposit funds into your cash account on time in order to meet your commitment.

This does not mean that you can meet your commitment whenever you feel like it, it just means that an extension of time is not applied for with the New York Stock Exchange but the five business days granted to eligible securities such as stock is applied to the trade.

In a nut sell you still must meet your commitment on a specified date and, if you fail to meet your commitment, it will be sold out at the stock brokerage company's discretion.

FACE VALUE/MARKET VALUE

When investors discuss their Financial Portfolio's with their stock-brokers or with anyone in general, it's quite easy to put a false value on the bond you may have long on your account. For example, let's assume that you have Five Thousand Highway Repair Muni Bonds long in your cash account.

Example:

Long: 5,000 Highway Repair 5 ¼ March 2003 @60

You may be inclined to say that your cash account has an equity value of Five Thousand Dollars but, Five Thousand Dollars is the *Face Value* of the Muni bond, not it's market value.

Further, you may miscalculate the market value of the Muni bond by calculating it's market value the way you calculate the market value of stock. The following examples will demonstrate how these common mistakes are made and how to calculate the market value of a Muni bond correctly.

Example 1a

5000 Highway Repair 5 ¼ March 2003 @60

The 5000 represents the Face Value of the Bond not the Market Value. The face value is the amount due the investor on maturity date.

Example 1b.

You may be inclined to calculate the Muni bonds market value the way you calculate your stocks market value. The following calculation is *Wrong*.

5000 Highway Repair 5 ¼ March 2003 @60

5000 (face value) x $60 (price per 1000 bonds)
=$30,000 INCORRECT

The correct way to calculate a Muni bond or any bond for that matter is to drop the last two zeros on the face value amount.

50 x $60 = $3,000 the correct market value for the Muni bond in our example is Three Thousand Dollars.

How Bonds Are Rated

Whether you're the type of investor that wants his/her investments as risk free as possible or, if you're the type of investor that likes high risk high gain investments, the bond market has a rating system that will ease your mind or excite the adventurer in you.

Bonds have ratings that vary from AAA to D. The following is a list of ratings and what they represent.

AAA—   Bonds with the AAA rating are of the highest grade. These bonds provide a high level of protection and security for both interest and principle pending. The prices of these bonds fluctuate (move up and down) only when interest rates fluctuate.

AA—   Bonds with the AA rating are considered high grade as well and differ in security in a very small degree.

A—   Bonds with the A rating are considered an upper medium type grade and are also considered to be very secure investments.

BBB—   Bonds with the BBB rating are of an average medium type rating. This rating is not as secure as the type A ratings because their prices fluctuate more with market or business conditions rather than interest rates.

BB—   Bonds with the BB rating are of a more lower medium rating. These are usually corporate bonds and fluctuate in price with the corporations economic standings.

B—   Bonds with the B rating are more speculative due to corporate market conditions. When times are tough, interest rates cannot be guaranteed.

CCC—   Bonds with CCC rating are of extreme speculation. They pay interest but it is not guaranteed.

CC—   Bonds with CC ratings are even more extreme speculation than the CCC rated bonds because you may be paid interest only when the issuer makes a profit.

C—   Bonds with C ratings state that they will only pay interest when the issuer makes a profit.

DDD—   Bonds with a D rating of any kind are bonds that are in default.

A Variety Of Bonds

There are a variety of bonds out there that you can invest in and, judging by the above rating chart, there is a variety of security and speculation to choose from. The following is a short rundown of the different types of bonds that are available to you for your investment ventures.

Bond (in general)– A Bond is a loan from you to the issuer of the bond and, in return, you get an IOU from the issuer to pay back the dept with interest on the maturity date of the issue that you choose to invest in.

Corporate Bonds– These are bonds issued by a corporation separate from that particular Corporations common stock.

Convertible Bonds– These are bonds that are eligible for exchange for common stock of the same corporation that issues the bond.

Junk Bonds– companies that are drowning in dept usually issue these bonds and may not be able to pay back the principal but pay very high interest rates.

Municipal Bond– These bonds are usually tax-exempt and issued by local government.

U.S. Treasury Bond–These are primarily long-term bonds with maturity dates anywhere from seven years to thirty years with fixed interest paid every six months

Bonds On Margin?

CAN I TRADE BONDS ON MARGIN?

Bonds, like eligible stocks, can be purchased on Margin. Although the requirements and releases differ greatly. Like eligible stocks, purchasing bonds on Margin can create Fed Calls if there is not enough equity to cover the purchase.

The biggest difference between stocks on Margin and bonds on Margin are the requirements. All eligible common stocks have a Margin requirement of fifty percent.

Bonds on the other hand have different Federal Requirements according to the type of issue they are. The following is a list of various bond issues and they're Federal Requirements, maintenance requirements and releases.

	Federal Requirements		Loan Value	Maintenance	Sales Release
U.S. Treasury	10%		90%	5%	10%
Muni Bonds	25%		75%	Depends on price	25%
Corp. Convertible	50%		50%	25%	50%
Corp. Non-Conv.	30%		70%	10 points	30%

FINANCIAL TERMS

Acquisition:

When one company acquires another company through a direct buy-out or through a hostile take over. A hostile take over can occur when one company acquires all the outstanding shares of another company thus owning controlling interest.

APR:

'Annual Percentage Rate': This is the cost of a loan reconfigured in the form of a percentage. Includes all fees including interest rates.

APY:

'Annual Percentage Yield': This is the interest earned on an investment in the form of a percentage. Example: $50 earned on a $1,000 investment is 5% (your ARY).

Annuity:

An annuity is simple an annual payment from an investment.

At The Market:

This term means to sell or buy stock at the current market price per share.

Ask Price:
This is the price per share that a broker is willing to sell a particular stock at.

Assets:
Anything that you own and are fully paid for and have a monetary value.

Baby Bonds:
These are bonds with a par value of less than $1,000.

Back End Load:
This term is referred to in terms of mutual fund investments when sales charges are deducted at the end of your investment when you sell it.

Bid Price:
This is the price per share of stock quoted to the stock investor when contemplating a purchase.

Bear Market:
A Bear Market represents a sell-off of stock during economically challenged times.

Bull Market:
This represents the stock investors buyers market when economic times are healthy.

Bearer Bond:
This is a non-registered bond which means that there is no record of ownership on file other than the person or organization physically holding the bond.

Beneficiary:

The recipient of assets from an investment such as an insurance policy or a will or simply the recipient of funds that have been directed to a specific party.

Block Trade:

When ten thousand shares of a stock are traded in a single transaction.

Blue Chip Stocks:

Financially secure companies that provide quality service and pay dividends to their investors. Note: dividends are not guaranteed like dividends issued on preferred stock.

Book Entry:

This is movement of a security that has no physical certificate or cash amount that does not involve physical currency exchanging hands.

Buy-In:

When a stock brokerage company is forced by rules and regulations to purchase to a security to cover a delinquent commitment.

Call Options:

The right to purchase a specified stock at a specified dollar per share amount. Also known as a stock option, Call Options have expiration dates.

Called Bond:

A Called Bond is a bond that has been called by the issuer. This means that the loan agreement is over and principle is paid off to the investor.

Capital:

Funds deposited to your cash account are considered capital as they are used for investment purposes as is stock deposited to your margin account to be used as collateral in order to purchase additional shares of stock.

Capital Gains:

Better known as profits, capital gains are realized when you sell a security for a dollar amount high that the dollar amount you paid for it at purchase.

Capital Loss:

Obviously the opposite of capital gains, Capital Lose is realized when you sell a security for less the dollar amount of which you purchased it.

Closing Price:

Final price per share of stocks at the closing bell at the Stock Exchanges on any given business day.

Collateral:

Any assets used to secure a loan by guaranteeing the lender that a loan will be covered incase of default.

Commissions:

Sales charge for services rendered by a stock broker or financial institution. Commissions are charged on both the Buy side and Sell side of the same security. This is a Win Win situation if you're a stock broker.

Commodity:

A commodity can be bulk goods or raw materials either used for consumption such as coffee, sugar, fruit, cocoa, soy and so on or for use in manufacturing merchandise such as metals, silver, gold etc. and even livestock are considered commodities.

Common Stock:

Common Stock s allows you as an investor to own shares of a corporation with the intention of profiting through market appreciation and /or dividends issued to the investor.

Convertible Bonds:

These are corporate bonds that convert to the issuing companies common stock at bond maturity.

Corporate Bonds:

These are bonds that are issued by corporations that are traded publicly.

Credit :

Credit is when you're extended the right to purchase 'anything' to be paid for at a latter time.

Credit Balance:

This is the amount of free funds in your cash account or margin account that you have or use toward the purchase of securities or money market funds.

Day Trade:

This is when the stock investor buys and sells the same security on the same day. Day trading in the cash account is not permitted, however, if you have a margin account with sufficient day trade buying power (usually for times the amount of the purchase side), you can day trade a security.

Debenture:
A Debenture is a corporate bond that is not backed by any collateral.Kown also as an unsecured bond.

Debit Balance:
A debit or debit balance is the amount of money owed to your account due to the purchase of stock or possibly an overpayment by your financial institution.

Debt:
A debt is an outstanding monetary obligation that you are held liable to pay back according to contract or other agreements.

Default:
An example of default is when an issued bond fails to pay principle and interest on its commitment to the investor.

Delivery:
When stock is shipped from one account to another account be form of journal entry or when stock is physically delivered off of your account to an designated destination.

Depreciation:
When anything of value decreases in said value. Example: when a stock selling for fifty dollars per share declines in value to thirty dollars per share.

Diversification:

A mix of different stocks, bonds mutual funds or any type of securities compiled to create a financial portfolio that should be able to avert a major loss in the event of a down market or depreciation of one of the securities being held on the portfolio.

Dividends:

Paying dividends is a way for corporations to distribute their earnings to investors. Dividends can be in the form of cash or additional shares of stock.

Dividend Reinvestment:

This is when a stock investor uses his/her dividends to purchase additional shares of said security issuing the dividend.

Equity:

Equity represents the value of assets owned in full by the investor. If you have an

Established cash account with a debit balance then the equity will be determined by subtracting the debit balance from the overall market value.

Escrow:

When funds or securities are held in escrow, they are being held by someone other than the investor or simple in a non-interest bearing account until a matter usually dictated by time, such as taxes, is resolved.

Estate:

This is the combined assets left behind by you the investor after you pass-on to a place where there *are* no taxes or death!

Estate Tax:
This is the amount of taxes owed on your estates gross assets after liabilities are deducted.

The Euro:
This represents the common currency shared by Austria, Belgium, Finland, France, Germany, Ireland, Italy, Luxembourg, Netherlands, Portugal and Spain.

Eurobonds:
These are bonds issued by countries trying to raise funds in other countries and using those other countries denominations.

Exchange:
You may be thinking that 'Exchange' is short for Stock Exchange and, your right except we are using the term 'Exchange' to describe a name change. Example: ABC Co. was acquired by XYZ Co. and all of the outstanding ABC Co. stock will now be exchanged for XYZ Co. stock. This could be a one for one Exchange meaning they take

Away one share of ABC Co. stock and replace it with one share of XYZ Co. stock for every share of ABC Co. stock owned or it could be a three for one Exchange and so on and adjusting the price per share accordingly.

Exercise:
When you act on your Right by terms of a contract.Example: Stock Options, if you exercise One Call of ABC Stock Option you are Exercising your 'Right' to purchase one hundred shares of ABC Co. stock.

Expiration Date:

This is the date that a stock option Call or Put will expire if you do not choose to exercise your Right accordingly to the terms of the option contract.

Face Value:

This is the value of an issued bond at maturity date and not the value of the bond on trade date.

Federal Funds:

When a bank or any other financial institution lends excess funds over night to other financial institutions. These funds are often used to wire funds between financial institutions and goes by the same name, Fed funds (wire funds).

Fiduciary:

This is an individual such as and executor (male) or executrix (female) or a financial institution that will hold and manage assets on the behalf of someone else.

Fixed Income:

This is when a person (usually retired) may be receiving and living off of the income of an investment such as a preferred stock or muni bond for example, that pay interest on a regular schedule.

Fractional Shares:

These are shares that are usually purchased when an investor has a dividend reinvestment plan or direct stock purchase plan that may not be able to apply all the funds available to purchase whole shares. Fractional shares will be purchased with the remaining funds available. These fractional shares will subsequently become whole shares when compiled.

Front End Load:
This is when you pay sales and/or service charges on an annuity or mutual fund on the day of purchase.

FNMA:
Federal National Mortgage Association pronounced 'Fannie Mae' is a corporation owned by shareholders that buys mortgages and resells them as securities on the open market.

GNMA:
Government National Mortgage Association, pronounced Ginnie Mae provide affordable mortgage funding for all and have investment securities that virtually risk free and have an attractive yield.

High Yield Bonds:
High yield bonds are typically junk bonds that pay out high yields to attract investors because of the high risk they have of defaulting.

In The Money:
This term is directed at stock option meaning that the strike price of the stock option is close or at the market price of the underlying stock and can be exercised.

Inflation:
Inflation is generally triggered by supply in demand. Which simply means that the demand for goods is greater that the supply available and triggers higher prices for goods.

Interest:
Interest is money paid for use of someone else's money or just the opposite, when someone pays you for the use of your money.

Issue:

This is when a corporation or government offers a new stock or bond to the public for the first time. The security itself is known as the 'Issue'.

Junk Bond:

These are bonds that carry a high yield to attract investors due to the fact that they a re of high risk and may default without warning.

Limit Order:

This is when you ask your stock-broker to buy or sell a certain security at a specific price per share when it is currently selling at another price per share. Your stock-broker won't have sit around starring at a quote machine waiting for the stock you requested a limit order on to reach your specified price per share. Your stock-broker can place an automatic limit order ticket in to buy or sell per your request, so don't forget that you have in that request or you may receive a surprise when the sale or buy goes off and you changed your mind two weeks before.

Long Position;

This is when you hold stock or bonds on your account that you may own one hundred percent or might have on margin. Although the securities may be being held on margin versus a debit balance, they are still considered long on the account.

Margin Account:

The margin account allows you to purchase stock buy depositing fifty per cent of the stocks market value or two thousand dollars, which ever is greater. The margin account also allows you to sell short and day trade if sufficient funds are available. If the value of your long securities on margin increase above the fifty per cent range, you can borrow the excess in the form of cash or purchase twice the value in stock. This is known as buying power.

Market Value:

The market value of a stock is calculated by the amount of shares long on the account times the current price per share. Example: if you own one hundred shares of

ABC Co, at thirty dollars per share your market value would be tree thousand dollars.

100 ABC Co. x $30 = $3,000.

Maturity Date:

This is the date that you agreed on with the issuer of a bond that your money could be invested with the issuer's corporation or government agency. On this date all principle and remaining interest payments will be paid to the investor.

New Issues (IPO):

When a stock or bond goes public for the first time, it's known as a new issue. IPOs or Initial Public Offering is when a private company goes public. These are also new issues.

No-Load:

A no-load mutual fund is a mutual fund purchased directly from the investment company that sponsors the fund.

Non-Callable:

This means that the issuer of the bond cannot redeem (or call) the bond before maturity date.

Odd Lot:

When you purchase or sell stock in denominations of less than one hundred shares it is considered an odd lot trade and may cost you a little extra in commissions.

Offering Price:

This is the price set by the underwriter when a stock is offered for sale to the public for the first time. The price per share may differ when it actually starts trading, it can be higher or lower.

OTC:

Over the counter stocks make up the majority of stocks trading in the United States. These stocks totaling over five thousand strong are listed on the Nasdaq Stock Market.

Portfolio:

When you have a cash or margin account that has more than one security long on it, regardless of whether it's stock or a bond or both, you have a portfolio.

Penny Stock:

Stocks that trade for under one dollar per share are penny stocks. If you invest in a penny stock and it's value increases sharply overnight, you may want to consider selling it ASAP because every other investor that has that stock will most likely be doing just that in order to take the profit.

Preferred Stocks:

These stocks are attractive to investors looking for annual income as the preferred stocks pay annual dividends on schedule. The only draw back is that preferred stock doesn't share in the market appreciation that its counter part common stock does when economic times are good.

Principle:
The principle is the amount owed on a bond (face value). In definition it also means the amount you owe on a loan.

Profit Taking:
When a stock increases sharply in price per share, many investors will start to sell off their shares in order to secure a profit. This is common practice in penny stock investing.

Put Option:
The right to sell a specified quantity of a specific stock at a specified price per share of that stock.

Stock Certificate:
This is the document that specifies the owner of a specified stock and a specified number of shares.

Street Name Stock:
Street name stock is stock that is held in the name of the institution that you do business with and is not in the form of a stock certificate with the owner of the shares printed on it's face.